I0492756

MONEYMAKER

more money & more free time

for YOU

MONEYMAKER

more money & more free time

for YOU

Jasmin Hajro

Jasmin Hajro

© 2017 Jasmin Hajro

All rights reserved

Cover design by Jasmin Hajro

First english edition 2018

ISBN-13: **978-1723096129**

ISBN-10: 1723096121

In this book you will discover 17 strategic actions:
the Moneymakers,
that you can implement immediately.
Which help you to earn more money &
have more free time.

Moneymaker 1. How to create multiple incomes.

Moneymaker 2. How to do well, by only doing 2 things

Moneymaker 3. What is your daily reading ?
The entrpreneurial bible of course.

Moneymaker 4. How to Build your Fortune, and still have enough time
for yourself, your family and your company.

Moneymaker 5. Orient yourself Globally

Moneymaker 6. How to save time with groceries.

Moneymaker 7. How to get into the Top 20%

Moneymaker 8. You & Direct mail

Moneymaker 9. How to fund yourself & save on your taxes

Moneymaker 10. How to connect your company to your community

Moneymaker 11. Your communication

Moneymaker 12. your blank book, the seminar

Moneymaker 13. how to use Social media correctly

Moneymaker 14. your email on autopilot

Moneymaker 15. How SEO isn't for you

16. Bonus moneymaker

17. Extra Bonus moneymaker

MONEYMAKER
more money & more free time
for you

From experience and
ready to implement ,
without BULLSHIT!

(So without theory
which looks great on paper & that in real life
maybe might work)

Only suitable for Entrepreneurs & self-employed

written by :

Jasmin Hajro, enterepreneur & author of:

Book How to Build up your own Fortuinje with simple steps, first edition.

Book Moneymaker.

Book Recipe for Happiness.

Book the lifebuoy for banks
" loyal banking "

book the Ultimate Winning Strategy
for entrepreneurs.

Book Poems, jokes and book.

Book Victory

Book Establishment Hajro, the conglomerate.

Book Victory II

book Always employment & always money in your pocket, every day.

Book Build your fortune, 3rd edition

Book Things you do not want to know.

Book Overcoming tough times

Book For you

Hi
my name is Jasmin Hajro.
I am the founder of Hajro Group (www.hajrobv.nl)
And the author of 13 books.
I am also the founder of the Giveth Life foundation.

Why is this Moneymaker for you?
Because I wish that when I started as an entrepreneur,
on December 17, 2012. That someone told me these things.
So that I had not wasted so much time,
and left so much money on the table.

This is for you, to save you time and money.

Briefly summarized, this book consists of
17 strategic actions,
with which you gain more profits and
more free time.

Moneymaker 1.

<u>**Your company's daughters.**</u>

**Give your current company a
number of subsidiaries.**

**Offer totally different
products & services.**

**This makes your company look
bigger in the eyes of the people.**

**And you can generate different income
streams for yourself.**

Moneymaker 2.

**The two things
on which you Must spend your time on, everyday.**

Which 2 are they?
Watch TV and be on Facebook?

Without BULLSHIT, so:
SALES & DIRECT MARKETING

If you sell something (sales),
then profits comes into your business.

If you become good at (direct marketing),
then profits comes into your business.

With marketing you save yourself time while selling.
You do not have to explain who
you are and what your company does.

How many hours per working day do you spend on sales?

How many hours per working day do You spend on Direct
Marketing?

WHAT HAPPENS IF YOU ONLY SPEND YOUR TIME ON
SALES &
DIRECT MARKETING ??

Will you have more profits
and therefore more money?

Sales & marketing are core of every business.
If you set everything aside and
just spend your workingdays on sales & marketing
You'll do good.

Moneymaker 3.

<u>the bible for entrepreneurs, written by an entrepreneur.</u>
<u>So it's your daily reading.</u>

No, it's not about GOD.
It says, written by an entrepreneur .....
YOU READ ONLY BOOKS WHICH ARE WRITTEN BY
PEOPLE
WHO OWN A COMPANY !!
Do you understand ?
This way you prevent feeding your mind with BULLSHIT.
And prevent yourself from modelling BULLSHIT.
So you save yourself time and money.

Ok then, now a bit about that Entrepreneurial Bible.
It is called No Excuses, the Power of self discipline
And is written by Brian Tracy
And yes, he has his own company.
Otherwise his name would not be here.

It comes down to self discipline.
And self discipline makes you feel very good
about yourself.
If you are going to exercise, for example, while most people are
watching TV.
If you to work on a Saturday,

while most people
have weekend.
If you take a step towards achieving your goals on Sunday.
The above 3 examples,
require discipline from you.

But 1, 3, 5 years from now where will you wind up?
And where will most people wind up?

Have you ever worked a day with pain because your teeth were
broken?

Have you ever worked with only 2 hours of sleep, the night before?
Have you ever worked without having slept the night before?

It was probably easier to watch TV then .....
But then I would be a Bullshitter for you, and not someone who you respect.

Oh yeah, buy the entrepreneurial bible.
NOW.

Moneymaker 4.

<u>Build your Fortune, and still have enough time for yourself, your family and your company.</u>

I'm not going to tell you this is the only way,
nor that it is the best way in the world.
I'm just telling you it's a way that works,
and with which you put money to work for you.

Because it takes little time, it is ideal.

So you'll still have plenty of time for yourself.
for your family. And of course enough time
for your company.

(This valuable book is for sale in 190 countries,
on 6 continents, worldwide. Get a copy at Kobo.com,
Amazon.com or at Barnes&Noble)

Moneymaker 5.

<u>Orient yourself globally</u>

Why would you have a region oriented company?
Like there is only a market for you in your city or state?

And like there are no prospects in other cities and states?
Who also spend money.

Think Global

The whole world is full of people who have money and spend
money.

So you are going to orient yourself Globally.

Oh yeah, in those other places
they also have email and mailboxes.

So with this we give birth to
(Your Company) GLOBAL

What did Donald Trump say?

If you're gonna do some thinking. Think BIG

Moneymaker 6.

Save time with groceries.

You know and have been through it:
making a shopping list,
going to the store,
searching for everything on your list and
putting it in your shopping Cart,
standing in line at the cash register,
waiting,
putting everything from the shoppingcart into your car,
driving home,
putting everything in the right spot.

Doing shopping every week.
Is a total of 8 hours that you spend per month.
Recognizable ? Of course, everyone does.

How do I say this neatly to you?
You're wasting your time, einstein.

From now on, you order your groceries.
When the Groceriestruck arrives at your door,
you feel rich and smart.

The 8 hours that you have saved,
you now spend on making profits.

Moneymaker 7.

the Top 20%

Some of them have prchased a set of greeting cards from me.

They live in those big, beautiful houses.

And often they have their own company.

You can read more about them in your entrepreneurial Bible.

Make sure that you get into that top group.

By becoming the best
in what you do.

Moneymaker 8.

You & Direct mail

Do you want to reach everyone?
Everyone has a mailbox.
So become very good at copywriting (selling in writing)
Learn and practice writing good sales letters.

Many people don't want to receive offers in the mail.

But you also deliver your sales letters to them,
because it is IMPORTANT that they know who you are,
what your company does. And that you REALLY exist.

After you have been sued,
then you can exclude them from your delivery list.
Only then.

Your mail is also Measurable,
you send out 100 letters, 20 people go to your website,
1 buys. That is measurable.

(Or you can have 1 million likes &
1 million engaged on social media.
Which is not measurable and brings you 0 dollar,
so it only costst you time)

Moneymaker 9.

<u>Fund yourself & save money on your taxes</u>

Go to a notary,
and make your company a Private Limited Company.
Then you pay less tax.
And you can sell shares, to fund yourself.

If you already have a Private Limited Company,
also go to the notary
to establish a foundation.
A foundation for your family,
to build a fortune in it.
Without having to pay taxes,
on that fortune.

Your foundation can also contribute to a better world,
in a way that you choose.

Moneymaker 10.

<u>Connect your company to your community</u>

When I buy from company A, I get a product and a receipt.

When I buy f rom companyB, I get the same product and I support
20 charities.

Where would you buy?

Support with 10% of your profits, the local charities and
good causes.
For your PR or for your soul.

(So that the people who work for those charities,
Become your customer.

Or so that your just feel great about yourself.

Or for both)

Moneymaker 11.

Your communication

Stick to mail & email.

**Everyone has a letterbox &
almost everyone has an email address**

**Social media platforms can
lose their popularity.
Like Hyves did.**

**Give people in your mail and email marketing
a reason to go to your website.
For example by giving away an ebook for free.**

Repetition is the name of the game.

**So you must Repeat at least every month
your mail & email marketing.**

Moneymaker 12.

your blank book, the seminar

Why would you pay 20 dollar for an empty book?
Because you are going to put some great ideas in it.
Do you know that 1 good idea can make you rich?

Buy an empty book. A journal
Then go to Youtube and listen to:
How to use a journal
from Jim Rohn.

To learn how to use your blank book,
and more information about your benefits
from using it.

(Yes, he also has his own company, which still exists after his death)

Moneymaker 13.

how to use Social media correctly

Social media is a waste of time

You can only use it as Leadgenerating Pages.

So on your facebook or linkedin you write :
A brief bio about you, a brief bio about your business,
the what you & your business can do for the visitor/prospect
and
a link to your website.

Just that,
after that you do not have to spend time on your social media
platforms anymore.
Never again.

Find me on LinkedIn, and you see an example
of the text that you will put on your social media.

If you're smart, you can spend your saved time
meaningfully
on those 2 things that will give you money.

Do you remember which 2 ???

SALES & MARKETING, Einstein

Moneymaker 14.

Your email on autopilot

If I receive a short email from you every week,
which states: hey, how is it?
How was your week ?
Have a nice weekend.
Greetings, You
There is a chance that after a certain period of time,
I will be open to buy something from you.

You know email marketing, look for a provider,
for example Mailchimp, set it up for the whole year.

And keep in touch with your potential customers.
Build stronger relationships &
send them offers.
On autopilot.
Without having to spend time on it.

Moneymaker 15.

<u>SEO is Not for you</u>

Why not ?

**If your website is: www.yourcompany.com
And someone opens his browser, and types into the
address bar
<u>www.yourcompany.com</u>**

Then he comes to your website, right?

**If someone goes to google.com and in Google types :
www.yourcompany.com , then he finds in
the search results a link to your website, right?**

**How did you want to measure SEO?
With a straightedge ?**

**When you become a medium-sized or large company,
with a large budget.
Go big,
with seo and other similar things.**

But not now.

**And you would spend your time on 2 other things, right?
Sales & marketing, remember?**

Are the Moneymakers valuable to you ?

Are you going to have more money and more free time?

Are you already implementing ????

If you are not serious about doing these things,
how will you make more money &
have more free time ?

Bonus Moneymaker 16.

Gratitude.

Be grateful for what you already have.

**Thank your customers &
thank the people who do something for you.**

**Also thank the people
who are always there for you.**

Bonus Moneymaker 17.

<u>Write your book or booklet.</u>

And position yourself as an expert.
If you know more about a subject than I do,
then you are an expert to me,
regarding that subject.

So write about what you are good at,
or what you know a lot about.

Describe your experiences as a salesperson,
or as an entrepreneur.

Describe your life lessons.

Then you publish your book,
via barnes&noble press & lulu.com &
createspace.com & kobo.com

Your book will then be available for sale in various
bookstores in several countries.
Including Amazon.com & barnes&noble

Your book becomes a marketing tool for you,
and for your company.

Mention in it or on your book, your web address or
that of your company.

Make yourself a familiar person.
People prefer to buy from a celebrity /
well-known person.

That's why you see celebrities and wellknown people
in advertisements,
praising products.

If you want to very easily create & publish your first book....

Then put all the texts on your website,
in a pdf.
Write and add some things, like your flyer and blogarticles.
And your first book is ready
to be published.
The advantage of this is that you have copyright
on the texts on your website and your other writings.
And,
you have went through the process of creating &
publishing a book already once.

So you can now more easily create your 2nd book .

Bonus Moneymaker 18.

Become really good at selling.

Read books about selling and
Go out selling door to door.

Become a master.

It does not matter that it takes years,
for you
to becomean expert salesperson or
to achieve mastery at selling.

If you become a 1000 times better at selling.
Then you will also earn a 1000 times better.

(What if you eventually build a team of 1000
salespeople and earn on every sale they make ?)

Thank you for reading these Moneymakers.

I know you will benefit from them,
if you implement them.

I wish you a lot more money &
a lot more free time.

God bless you,

Jasmin Hajro
© 2018

P.S. Money is just paper, ink and metals.

P.P.S. Success in business can only be measured with dollars.
Have you sold things and earned 2000 dollar this month,
then you're having a successful month. And you are successful.

P.P.P.S Hopefully money and success are no longer
mysterious to you.

By buying this book,
you made a donation to
foundation Giveth Life
&
40 other charities.

Thank you.

I wish you a lot moneymaking.

Recommended books to read:

the books of Joe Girard

the books of Brian Tracy

the books of Dan S. Kennedy

all books about sales that
you can find.

The Ultimate Winning Strategy,
for entrepreneurs by Jasmin Hajro

Only taking action will give you :

www.ingramcontent.com/pod-product-compliance
Lightning Source LLC
Chambersburg PA
CBHW071201220526
45468CB00003B/1111